1

AMAZING REPTILES

Sea Turtles

by Nancy Furstinger

Content Consultant
Michael Frick
Teaching Lab Specialist
University of Florida

Core Library

An Imprint of Abdo Publishing
www.abdopublishing.com

www.abdopublishing.com

Published by Abdo Publishing, a division of ABDO, PO Box 398166,
Minneapolis, Minnesota 55439. Copyright © 2015 by Abdo Consulting
Group, Inc. International copyrights reserved in all countries. No part of
this book may be reproduced in any form without written permission from
the publisher. Core Library™ is a trademark and logo of Abdo Publishing.

Printed in the United States of America, North Mankato, Minnesota
042014
092014

Cover Photo: Epic Stock Media/Shutterstock Images
Interior Photos: Epic Stock Media/Shutterstock Images, 1; Brian J.
Skerry/National Geographic Image Collection/Glow Images, 4; Cigdem
Sean Cooper/Shutterstock Images, 7, 43; NHPA/SuperStock, 8; Richard
Whitcombe/Shutterstock Images, 10; Shutterstock Images, 11, 31; David
Fleetham/VWPics/Newscom, 12; Michael Krabs/Glow Images, 15; Olivier
Blaise/Zumapress.com/Newscom, 17; Kjersti Joergensen/Shutterstock
Images, 19; Andrey Nekrasov/VW Pics/SuperStock, 20; Mark A. Johnson/
Corbis/Glow Images, 23, 45; Salvador Serrano/Shutterstock Images, 25;
NaturePL/SuperStock, 26; Sergey Popov V/Shutterstock Images, 28; Red
Line Editorial, 33; Minden Pictures/SuperStock, 34; Matthias Graben/Glow
Images, 37; Tyrone Turner/National Geographic Image Collection/Glow
Images, 39

Editor: Mirella Miller
Series Designer: Becky Daum

Library of Congress Control Number: 2014932341

Cataloging-in-Publication Data
Furstinger, Nancy.
  Sea turtles / Nancy Furstinger.
    p. cm. -- (Amazing reptiles)
Includes bibliographical references and index.
ISBN 978-1-62403-375-9
1. Sea turtles--Juvenile literature.   I. Title.
597.92/8--dc23

                                                        2014932341

CONTENTS

The Remarkable Sea Turtle

A leatherback sea turtle glides through the warm waters of the Gulf of Mexico. The giant reptile spots a jellyfish near the surface of the water. The jellyfish's deadly tentacles trail behind its body, ready to sting predators or prey. But the hungry leatherback is not afraid. It uses its powerful flippers to steer through the water toward the jellyfish. After quickly reaching its prey, the leatherback opens

Leatherbacks are the largest of the sea turtle breeds. These turtles need to eat twice their body weight per day.

its scissors-like jaws and chomps into the jellyfish. Long spines inside the leatherback's mouth spear the slippery prey. The jellyfish struggles and waves its tentacles, trying to sting the leatherback. It is no use. Thick skin protects the leatherback. The turtle uses its strong throat muscles to swallow the jellyfish.

After finishing its prey, the leatherback swims away in search of its next meal.

Sea Turtles vs. Land Turtles

Sea turtles live in most saltwater oceans around the world. Tortoises are also found around the world. Tortoises rarely go in the water. They walk around on legs. Sea turtles swim using flippers. Female sea turtles nest in the same regions where they were born. Tortoises have small home ranges, so many may return to the nest site where they were born.

Sea Turtle Species

The leatherback is one of seven sea turtle species in the world. The others include the flatback, green, hawksbill, Kemp's ridley, loggerhead, and olive ridley sea turtles. These reptiles vary in size, color, appearance, and

Green sea turtles can grow to be up to five feet (1.5 m) long.

sometimes habitat. But all sea turtles spend almost their entire lives in the ocean.

The leatherback is the largest sea turtle species in the world. Some leatherbacks measure approximately seven feet (2 m) long. This is the size of a small car! Leatherbacks can weigh as much as 2,000 pounds (907 kg). The largest leatherback on record stretched eight and a half feet (2.6 m) long. Its flippers spanned

A Kemp's ridley turtle's shell usually measures between 24 and 28 inches (61 to 71 cm).

eight feet (2.4 m) long. The turtle weighed in at 2,020 pounds (916 kg).

The smallest sea turtle species is the Kemp's ridley. They weigh between 80 and 100 pounds (36 and 45 kg).

Ancient Survivors

Sea turtles have lived on Earth for approximately 245 million years. They were around before the dinosaurs. The species that would evolve into sea turtles were once land creatures. They roamed the land, hunting prey. These land turtles gradually evolved to live in water, where they could find prey more easily. Sea turtles continue to lay their eggs on land, however.

Similar Features

Sea turtles still have some of the same features as their early ancestors. Flippers and a shell are two of these features. Early sea turtles developed flippers that helped them move through the water. A sea turtle's front flippers are broad and flat. Back flippers act like rudders and help a turtle steer through the water.

Most sea turtles have two hard shells. The shells are flat and streamlined. This lets the turtles glide quickly through the water. The top shell is called the

Giant Slurper

In 2013 scientists in Morocco discovered the remains of a giant sea turtle that lived approximately 67 million years ago. The turtle had a large skull and a tube-like snout. Scientists think this turtle used suction feeding to adapt from living on land to spending most of its life in water. It used its long snout like a straw. This prehistoric creature sucked down prey such as jellyfish.

A sea turtle's front flippers act like arms and allow it to swim fast.

carapace. It is made of bones. The carapace protects sea turtles' backs. Tough plates called scutes cover the carapace. Sea turtles also have a bottom shell, called the plastron. It protects their internal organs.

The leatherback is the only sea turtle that does not have a hard shell. Thick leather covers its back instead. This leather runs in rubbery ridges down the turtle's body.

Scute

Flipper

Carapace

Beak

Flipper

Plastron

Flippers

Sea Turtle Body Parts
Chapter One discusses many sea turtle body parts. This
diagram shows some of the physical characteristics of a sea
turtle. How might some of these parts help a sea turtle eat
prey? How might other body parts protect a sea turtle
from predators?

The seven species of sea turtles have a range of
colors. The leatherback is dark gray or black. Flatback,
olive ridley, and Kemp's ridley turtles have greenish-
gray shells. The loggerhead has a reddish-brown shell.
The hawksbill has a patterned shell of brown and red.
The green sea turtle does not have a green shell.
Instead, it is brown or olive-colored.

CHAPTER TWO

Amazing Life Cycles

Scientists are not sure how long sea turtles live in the wild. It is not easy to determine the age of these reptiles. Scientists are still studying their life spans. They think some sea turtles could live up to 150 years. This would make them one of the longest-living animals on Earth.

It is rare to see two sea turtles together outside of mating season.

Finding a Mate

Most sea turtles prefer to live alone. However, males and females come together during mating season. Mating season ranges from March through October, depending on the species. Sea turtles begin mating at different ages. Some species become parents for the first time at ten years old. Others wait to mate until they are 50 years old!

Weeping Mother Turtles

Female sea turtles appear to be crying tears as they crawl ashore to nest. They are not really crying but shedding saltwater. A special gland near the eyes rids the turtle's body of extra salt from drinking ocean water. This sticky stream of tears helps keep the turtle's eyes free of sand while she digs her nest.

Male sea turtles court females. They become jealous if another male competes for a female's attention. Males will even fight one another for a female. The males bite one another on the flippers and tail. Even so, some females mate with more than one male during mating season.

A female green sea turtle digs a nest in the sand with her back flippers.

Building a Nest

Female sea turtles must come ashore to bury their eggs. They return to the same region where they hatched to dig their nests. Six of the sea turtle species dig their nests at night. Kemp's ridley females dig their nests during the day.

When a female is finished digging, she places her tail over the nest opening and lays her eggs. A female will lay a clutch, or group, of 70 to 190 eggs, depending on her species. The eggs are approximately the size of golf balls. They are soft and slippery, so they do not break when they land in the nest. The female covers her eggs with sand and moves back to the ocean. She will return within 12 to 14 days to lay her next clutch. Sea turtles can nest two to four times each season. Loggerhead females nest up to five times each season. After nesting many times in one season, female sea turtles wait two to three years before nesting again.

Five species of sea turtles nest alone. But the olive and Kemp's

Built-In GPS

How does a female sea turtle find the region in which she was born? Scientists believe female turtles use Earth's magnetic fields to plot their courses. This guides them hundreds or thousands of miles to the right regions. Smelling certain odors carried by ocean currents also helps guide the turtles.

This small Costa Rican beach is flooded with olive ridley sea turtles each year.

ridley sea turtles arrive at the beach in large groups. Their arrival is called an *arribada*. This is the Spanish term for "arrival." The biggest known arribada took place on a Costa Rican beach in 1995. Approximately 500,000 olive ridley females streamed ashore!

Baby Sea Turtles

Sea turtle eggs incubate for 50 to 60 days. If the temperature of the nest is warm, most of the turtles will be females. A cool nest will yield mostly males. The hatchlings break open their shells using a sharp egg tooth. The egg tooth is on the end of the hatchlings' snouts. Then the babies dig upward through the sand together. This may take a few days.

The hatchlings leave their nests at night. They look like their parents but measure only one to two inches (3 to 5 cm) long. The hatchlings search for a bright horizon, usually the moon and stars reflecting off the water.

The turtles race to the ocean. As they scramble across the sand, baby turtles must dodge predators such as birds and crab. Once in the ocean, they need to escape hungry fish that prey on turtles.

Only 1 out of 1,000 hatchlings will live to become an adult sea turtle.

EXPLORE ONLINE

The focus in Chapter Two is the life cycle of sea turtles. It also touches on several dangers hatchlings face. The website below discusses how scientists help threatened sea turtles' nests. As you know, every source is different. How is the information given in the website different from the information given in this chapter? How is it the same? What new information can you learn from this website?

Turtle Eggs
www.mycorelibrary.com/sea-turtles

CHAPTER THREE

Cold-Blooded Reptiles

Sea turtles are cold-blooded, which means they cannot control their body temperatures. They take on the temperature of their surroundings instead. Swimming in warm water keeps turtles from getting too cold. Leatherbacks are so large and dark-colored that they are able to absorb much of their heat from the sun. They store this energy in fat

Sea turtles must swim to the water's surface to breathe air into their lungs.

tissue. Leatherbacks in the Caribbean Sea sometimes overheat and swim deeper to cool down.

Swimming and Diving

Sea turtles are strong swimmers. These reptiles are also excellent divers. Leatherbacks can dive to depths of 3,900 feet (1,189 m) to hunt for jellyfish. They breathe air through their lungs. Sea turtles can also hold their breath for long periods. Green sea turtles can stay underwater for up to five hours. Their heart rate slows when they do this. They can go up to nine minutes between heartbeats!

Staying Safe

Sea turtles have dry, scaly skin. Their skin has special coloration that protects them from predators. Scientists call this coloration countershading. A sea turtle's top shell is darker than its bottom shell. The top shell is usually swirled with colors and patterns to blend in with sea plants. A tiger shark swimming near the water's surface would not see the turtle. The

Green sea turtles can move at speeds of up to 1.5 miles (2.2 km) per hour.

dark top shell blends in with the deep ocean water. Predators swimming below a sea turtle will not see the turtle either. The light bottom shell blends in with the bright sky above. These features also keep a turtle hidden from its potential prey. Unlike land turtles, sea turtles cannot pull their heads and flippers into their shells for protection.

Sharp Senses

Sea turtles have strong senses. Their sense of smell is especially powerful. Sea turtles pull in water through their noses and push it out through their mouths. This helps turtles sniff out food and predators. Sea turtles can also see clearly underwater. They are nearsighted out of water, however. Sea turtles have good hearing. Their ears are inside of their heads. They use them to hear low-pitched sounds. They can also pick up sound vibrations. Sea turtles can sense touch on their flippers and their shells.

Diet

A sea turtle hunts using its toothless jaws. The jaws end in a beak. This beak lets the turtle grab, snip, or crush food depending on its diet.

Sea turtles hunt for food during the day. Most young turtles eat plankton or other small, floating animals. Adult turtles eat a combination of sea plants and fish. They also snack on fish eggs.

The seven species of sea turtles have different diets. Leatherbacks hunt jellyfish. At night they feed in the upper waters, where jellyfish gather. When the

A hawksbill sea turtle breaks coral apart with its beak.

sun rises, leatherbacks must dive as the jellyfish move deeper.

Some species dive all the way down to the ocean floor to find hard-shelled prey. Hawksbills eat coral and squid. Loggerheads crush snails and clams. Olive ridleys eat crab and shrimp. Kemp's ridleys enjoy blue crab.

A green sea turtle eats plants and algae off the bottom of the ocean floor.

Cleaning Stations

In Hawaii green sea turtles swim up to cleaning stations. These are like underwater car washes for turtles. A crew of yellow tang fish nibbles algae off the turtles' shells until they are clean. The fish also eat harmful pests that have taken a ride on the turtles' shells. Both species benefit from these cleanings. The fish get a healthy snack. And the turtles leave with smoother shells, making it easier to swim.

Other species graze in shallow water and in coral reefs. Flatback sea turtles feed on sea cucumbers and squid. Green sea turtles eat mostly sea grasses. Their saw-like beaks let them cut these plants. These turtles are like underwater lawn mowers!

All sea turtles are specially adapted to catch their favorite prey. Biologist Blair Witherington describes how the Kemp's ridley sea turtle is a small but mighty force when it comes to hunting blue crab:

The largest Kemp's ridley is just small enough for a strong person to pick one up and carry it. But in doing so, one might find oneself slapped, bitten, and generally regretful for the attempt. Although Kemp's ridley is small relative to the other sea turtles, their scrappy nature makes them seem comparatively substantial. Kemp's ridleys are fast and mean. Certainly, having to deal with a face full of darting, slashing blue crab during every meal would favor those both nimble and determined.

Source: Blair Witherington. Sea Turtles: An Extraordinary Natural History of Some Uncommon Turtles. *Minneapolis: Voyageur Press, 2006. Print. 107.*

Back It Up

Blair Witherington is using evidence to support a point. Write a paragraph describing the point Witherington is making. Then write down two or three pieces of evidence Witherington uses to make the point.

CHAPTER FOUR

Tropical Waters

Sea turtles live in oceans around the world. Most of these habitats have tropical or temperate waters. Most species live and hunt for food in the waters that border beaches. Sea turtles live in bays, lagoons, and coral reefs. These coastal waters contain a rich mix of sea plants and prey.

The leatherback sea turtle is an exception to this rule. These turtles also hunt for prey in cold

Sea turtles survive in saltwater habitats around the world.

waters. Their size and a layer of fat help leatherbacks conserve body heat. They have the broadest range of any reptile. Their range in the Atlantic Ocean is as far north as Canada and Norway. To the south, their range extends to the tip of South America. Leatherbacks can also be found in the warmer waters of the Atlantic, Pacific, and Indian oceans, as well as in the Mediterranean Sea.

Green sea turtles live in the warm waters of the Atlantic, Pacific, and Indian oceans. Unlike other sea turtle species, some green turtles visit land for more than just nesting. They crawl up onto beaches to sunbathe.

Migrations Near and Far

Most sea turtles migrate long distances between their feeding grounds and the beaches where they nest. Leatherbacks have the longest migration routes. Some swim more than 3,000 miles (4,828 km) between their nesting and feeding grounds! Flatbacks, on the other hand, only migrate between 134 to 807 miles (216 to 1,299 km) around the northern coast of Australia.

A green sea turtle sunbathes on a beach in Hawaii.

Hawksbills prefer the same warm coastal waters as green turtles. They hunt in coral reefs, where sponges are plentiful.

The small population of Kemp's ridley turtles lives mostly in the Gulf of Mexico. They also range along the Atlantic Ocean from Cape Cod, Massachusetts,

Tracking Sea Turtles

In the past, scientists used numbered tags placed on turtles' front flippers to track them. People who saw turtles would read the tags and send letters to the scientists. But this method only offered information about where the turtles nested. And people could only see the tags when the turtles were on land. Now scientists glue radio transmitters to the shells of the turtles they are trying to track. These transmitters track migration routes. They deliver location data to satellites. The satellites then send the information to the scientists.

down to Florida. These turtles stay in shallow waters where they can feast on crab.

Olive ridley turtles live in the tropics. They live in the southern Atlantic, Pacific, and Indian oceans. They prefer the open ocean to the coastline.

Of all the sea turtle species, loggerheads are present in the greatest quantity in US waters. They have a huge range in both the Atlantic and Pacific oceans. Loggerhead turtles also live in the Indian Ocean.

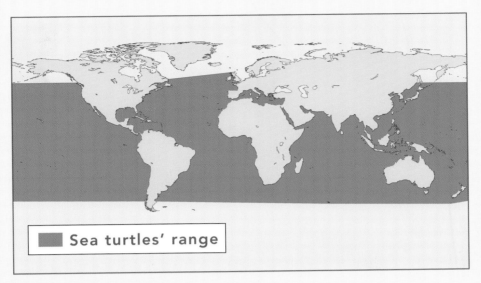

Sea turtles' range

Sea Turtles' Range

Almost all sea turtles live in warm ocean waters. This map shows where all seven species of sea turtles live. Why are these habitats best suited for sea turtles? Write a few sentences about what makes these habitats ideal for sea turtles' feeding and nesting habits.

They travel from coastal waters out to sea in search of food.

Flatbacks have the smallest range of all the sea turtles. They stick to tropical waters between Australia and New Guinea. They do not migrate across the open ocean like other species.

CHAPTER FIVE

Many Risks

Six of the seven sea turtle species are in danger of extinction. Only the flatback sea turtle is not at risk. The Kemp's ridley is the most endangered sea turtle. Only approximately 1,000 nesting females exist worldwide. Along with the hawksbill, leatherback turtles are critically endangered. The loggerhead and green sea turtle are also endangered species.

The hawksbill sea turtle is a critically endangered species.

Sea turtles face threats before they even hatch. Predators such as raccoons dig up and feast on turtle eggs. Hatchlings deal with even more dangers as they race to the ocean. Fish and pelicans gobble baby turtles that reach the ocean. Tiger sharks and saltwater crocodiles prey upon turtles as they grow.

Human-Made Threats

Humans are the biggest threat to sea turtles. Laws protect sea turtles in most countries. But poachers continue to collect eggs from turtle nests. They also hunt turtles for their body parts. Their meat is turned into turtle steaks. The skin from olive ridley

One Flipper

One unlucky green sea turtle named Allison lost three flippers to a shark. But Allison's luck changed when Sea Turtle, Inc., rescued her. This conservation group brought Allison to their rehabilitation center. At first she could only swim in circles with her one remaining flipper. Then an intern designed a special jacket for Allison. The jacket has a large flipper on the top. Now Allison can swim with other rescued turtles!

Turtle egg collectors wait on a Costa Rican beach for female turtles to arrive and lay their eggs.

turtles is sold for leather. Hawksbill shells are carved into jewelry.

Some sea turtles are caught by accident. Fishing nets meant to capture fish entangle turtles. The turtles often drown, unable to reach the surface to breathe.

Human activities also endanger sea turtles. Off-road vehicles sometimes disturb turtle nests. In the water, boats can collide with turtles. Their propellers injure turtles swimming near the surface.

Pollution is also deadly for sea turtles. Garbage on the shore and in the water can kill turtles. Leatherbacks mistake balloons and plastic bags for jellyfish and eat them. Toxic chemicals dumped by factories can end up in the ocean. Light pollution from car lights or beachfront houses causes nesting sea turtles and hatchlings to become confused. They head toward these artificial lights instead of the ocean.

Habitat loss is another problem. People build resorts and docks on the beaches where sea turtles nest. This leaves less room for turtles to dig their nests.

Protecting Sea Turtles

Conservation groups are working to make sure sea turtles survive in the wild. They help scientists gather turtle eggs and relocate them to safer beaches. Other eggs are hatched in hatcheries. The hatchlings are released immediately upon hatching.

Toxins from oil spills in the ocean can kill sea turtles.

Countries around the world are protecting the places where sea turtles nest. During nesting season, many hotels, shops, and restaurants near beaches turn off their lights. This allows nesting female sea turtles to find the ocean after laying their eggs.

Tourists travel to Costa Rica and other regions to observe sea turtles in the wild. Local guides bring small groups to the beach. Visitors watch nesting turtles. Some return in seven to eight weeks to watch the hatchlings race to the sea. This kind of travel is called ecotourism. These tourists bring money into the regions they visit. Ecotourism can convince local people to protect sea turtles instead of harvesting them.

It is not too late to save sea turtles. None of the seven species have disappeared yet. Humans must protect sea turtles' habitats and nesting grounds. Then these ancient reptiles will continue to survive in the wild for years to come!

FURTHER EVIDENCE

Chapter Five gives information about threats to sea turtles. What was one of the chapter's main points? What are some pieces of evidence in the chapter that support this main point? Check out the website at the link below. Find some information on this website that supports the main point in this chapter. Write a few sentences explaining how the information from the website supports the chapter's main point.

Turtles in Trouble
www.mycorelibrary.com/sea-turtles

Christopher Columbus landed on the Caribbean island of Las Tortugas, part of the Cayman Islands, in May 1503. It seemed overloaded with sea turtles. Marine biologist James Spotila explains how the turtle population has changed since then:

When Christopher Columbus first saw the Cayman Islands he was steering his ship through a sea of turtles. His son Ferdinand wrote, "We sighted two very small low islands full of turtles (as was all the sea thereabouts, so that it seemed to be full of little rocks); that is why these islands were called Las Tortugas." The turtle population appeared to be inexhaustible to the generations of hunters supplying meat to passing ships. A few centuries later, however, the turtles of Las Tortugas were gone.

Source: James Spotila. Sea Turtles: A Complete Guide to Their Biology, Behavior, and Conservation. Baltimore: John Hopkins University Press, 2004. Print. 73.

Changing Minds

Take a position on turtle fishing in the Cayman Islands. Imagine your best friend has the opposite opinion. Write a paper trying to change your friend's mind. Make sure you explain your opinion and your reasons for it. Include facts and details that support your reasons.

Common Name: Sea turtle

Scientific Names: *Dermochelyidae* (leatherbacks) and *Chelonioidea*

Average Size: Two to seven feet (1 to 2 m) long, depending on species

Average Weight: 80 to 2,000 pounds (36 to 907 kg), depending on species

Color: Dark gray, black, greenish-gray, reddish-brown, brown, olive, and cream

Average Life Span: Up to 100 years in the wild

Diet: Plankton, fish, fish eggs, sponges, hard-shelled sea creatures, squid, jellyfish, and sea grasses

Habitat: Saltwater oceans

Predators: Humans, raccoons, crab, vultures, fish, pelicans, tiger sharks, and crocodiles

Did You Know?

- Young hawksbill, loggerhead, and green sea turtles cannot dive to deep ocean waters, so they live among floating sea plants.
- Sea turtles' shells are covered in plates so tough that most sharks cannot bite through them.
- Sea turtles have special glands that remove salt from the saltwater they take in.

Say What?

Learning about sea turtles can mean learning a lot of new vocabulary. Find five new words in this book that you've never seen or heard before. Use a dictionary to find out what they mean. Using your own ideas, write down the meaning of each word. Then use each word in a sentence.

Another View

There are many different sources of information about sea turtles. As you know, every source is different. Ask a librarian or another adult to help you find a reliable source about sea turtles. Write a short essay comparing and contrasting the new source's point of view with the ideas in this book. How are the sources similar? How are the sources different? Why do you think they are similar or different?

Why Do I Care?

This book discusses why it is important to keep sea turtle species from becoming extinct. Even if you don't live near sea turtles, why should you care about protecting them? Write down two or three reasons humans should care about sea turtle populations.

Surprise Me

Learning about sea turtles can be interesting and exciting. Think about what you learned from this book. Can you name two or three facts about sea turtles that you found surprising? Write a short paragraph about each fact. Why did you find these facts surprising?

GLOSSARY

carapace
the top shell of a turtle

cold-blooded
unable to regulate body
temperature without an
outside source, such as
the sun

ecotourism
environmentally responsible
travel to natural areas

endangered
threatened with extinction

extinction
the death of all members of
a species

plankton
tiny animals and plants
that float near the surface
of the sea

plastron
the bottom shell of a turtle

poachers
people who catch wild
animals illegally

scutes
tough plates covering a
turtle's shell

LEARN MORE

Books

Marsh, Laura. *Sea Turtles*. Washington, DC: National Geographic Children's Books, 2011.

Molnar, Michael. *Green Sea Turtles*. Mankato, MN: Smart Apple Media, 2011.

Swinbrune, Stephen. *Turtle Tide: The Ways of Sea Turtles*. Honesdale, PA: Boyds Mills Press, 2010.

Websites

To learn more about Amazing Reptiles, visit **booklinks.abdopublishing.com**. These links are routinely monitored and updated to provide the most current information available.

Visit **www.mycorelibrary.com** for free additional tools for teachers and students.

INDEX

ABOUT THE AUTHOR

Nancy Furstinger is the author of more than 100 books. She has worked as an editor at children's book publishing houses. She rescues painted and snapping turtles that wander along the road in her lakeside community.

DATE DUE

MAY 2 1 2015		
JUL 0 7 2015		
		PRINTED IN U.S.A.